SWEET-ASS AFFIRMATIONS COLORING BOOK
FOR YOUR CREATIVE MANIAC MIND

Rage Create®

YO, RAGE CREATOR!

Merci. Gracias. Grazie. Danke.

Thank you for playing with the Sweet-Ass Affirmations Coloring Book!

We created this coloring book (alongside the Sweet-Ass Affirmations card decks) so you can get jiggy with daily affirmations in your own creative and colorful ways.

We are honored to co-create with you!

FREE BONUS PACK: Special Offer For You

To show our thanks for supporting this project, we've created a pack of free digital goodies for you, including:

- All 60 High-Resolution Affirmation Cards in Digital Format (front and back)
- Desktop and Mobile Wallpaper Backgrounds for Each Card!
- Print-at-home Affirmation Card Pack so you can make your own deck at home

DOWNLOAD YOUR FREE BONUS ITEMS HERE:
RAGECREATE.COM/COLORBONUS

OR SCAN THIS QR CODE: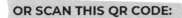

20% off on your Sweet-Ass Affirmations Card Deck

We just can't help ourselves, so here are more treats! Here is a 20% off coupon to the *Sweet-Ass Affirmations: Motivation for Your Creative Maniac Mind* affirmation decks.

You can redeem at RageCreate.com:
Promo code: **COLORBONUS20**

If you encounter any issues with your order or just want to send us your love, send us an email at hello@ragecreate.com.

To space!
Skid the Unisquid and the Rage Create Maniacs

DISCLAIMER AND COPYRIGHT

Disclaimer

The information provided within this publication is for general informational purposes only. While we try to keep the information up-to-date and correct, there are no representations or warranties, express or implied, about the completeness, accuracy, reliability, suitability or availability with respect to the information, products, services, or related graphics contained in this publication for any purpose. Any use of this information is at your own risk.

The methods and advice described within this book are the creator's personal thoughts, recommendations, and experiences. They are not intended to be a definitive set of instructions for this project or you.

The authors do not assume and hereby disclaim any liability to any party for any loss, damage, or disruption caused by errors or omissions, whether such errors or omissions result from accident, negligence, or any other cause. If you wish to apply ideas contained in this publication, you are taking full responsibility for your actions.

All information, content, and material in this publication and all content affiliated is for informational purposes only.

Copyright

ISBN: 978-1-7363287-1-2
Designed by RAGE CREATE LLC
Written by Heath Armstrong and Jason Berwick

© Copyright 2022 RAGE CREATE LLC
All Rights Reserved (for pizza parties too)
Published by RAGE CREATE LLC

No part of this publication may be reproduced or transmitted in any form or by any means, electronic or mechanical, including photocopying, recording or by any information storage and retrieval system, without written permission from the publisher and author.

For inquiries about permissions for reproducing parts of this guide and journal, please e-mail: hello@ragecreate.com

For more information, visit our website at Ragecreate.com

A TRANSMISSION FROM URANUS: A MESSAGE FROM THE CREATORS

"Every child is an artist; the problem is staying an artist when you grow up."

- Pablo Picasso

Experts have touted the benefits of adult coloring books for years. Coloring kicks the nefarious tushies of stress gremlins, centers you, improves your focus, and even helps induce mindfulness. It's an awesome restorative activity, and a great learning and self-improvement opportunity as well.

Of course, Skid and the Unisquids want to kick things up a notch, so we won't just have you coloring a bunch of nonsensical doodles. Instead, you'll be working on coloring sheets which contain powerful, unfiltered, and hilarious affirmations from the Sweet-Ass Affirmations decks. So, as you color, we'll be filling you with jetpacks of motivation so that you can rediscover your inner child, unleash the creative beast within you, and rage forward toward your visions! High-five!

Grab your crayons or coloring pencils and enjoy this wild ride! Don't hold back, okay? Sic your five-year-old self on this wacky canvas and color *outside* the lines.

WHAT'S INSIDE!

A Transmission from Uranus: A Message from the Creators.............page 5

Love Yo Self, Foo!: Color Your Way to Self Empowerment

I Love and Respect Myself...page 11
I Give No Fucks, I Kiss No Butts ....page 13
I Control My Flows...page 15
Exceptional, Optimal and Serene..page 17
My Bling Is Priceless...page 19
The Greatest Miracle in the World...page 21
Happy and Free ....page 23
The Best Fucking Life Ever...page 25
Experience the World ....page 27
My Financial Status Does Not Dictate My Happiness......................page 29

Building Your Sexy-Ass Self: Take Care of Dat Ass

I Am A Child of Nature...page 33
The Superfoods: Strength, Resilience, Prosperity............................page 35
My Body Is My Sanctuary...page 37
Heal My Desires and Wants ....page 39
I Decorate My Life ....page 41
I Make Peace with the World...page 43

Prepping for Launch: Building the Rage Creator Mindset

Emotional Fear is an Illusion...page 47
I Am the Hero in My Own Video Game...page 49
I Am the Star of the Movie of My Life..page 51
One with My Desires ....page 53
My Desires Are on Its Way to Me at Warp Speed ....page 55
I Am an Animal of the Earth...page 57
I Am the World...page 59
Nothing Can Stop Me from World Domination................................page 61
Nothing Can Stop Me from Victory..page 63
I Never Stop Peaking..page 65
Focused on What Lights Me Up ....page 67
I Sail to My Treasures ....page 69
IDGAF about Stress ....page 71

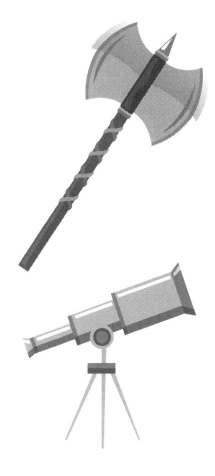

Unleashing the Power of Creation

I Am an Ax-Wielding Warrior..page 75
I Overcome All Conflicts ....page 77
I Rage Create Solutions ....page 79
I Never Stop Rage Creating ....page 81
I Am Unique in My Offerings ....page 83
I Honor My Creative Process ....page 85
I Push Myself to Learn..page 87
I Am A Soldier of Persistence...page 89
My Life Is Simple and Focused ....page 91
I Show Up to Hunt and I Eat...page 93
I Am Immortal Through My Creations ....page 95
The Superstar I Am Becoming ....page 97
I Respect and Honor My Current Work...page 99
I Surround Myself with Inspirational People.....................................page 101
I Paint My Lemons in Gold...page 103
I Rage in the Rain...page 105
I Exercise my Happiness Muscle Everyday.......................................page 107
I Am One with My Vision..page 109

Enjoy Yo' Self: It's A Celebration!

Everyday Is a Bonus Round...page 113
I Am A Champion of the Sun ....page 115
I Am My Own Lottery Ticket ....page 117
I Live My Life as if I Have to Live It Over Again................................page 119
I Electrify My Relationship with Life...page 121
Every Breath Is a Chest Full of Treasure..page 123
This Moment Is My Awesome Life ....page 125
I Give to Others ....page 127
I Create Happiness...page 129
I Develop Within the Experience ....page 131
Today I am 1% Better...page 133
My Moments Turn Out the Best ....page 135
The Best Experiences of the Past ....page 137

Achievement Unlocked: Share Your Colored Affirmations and Win! .....page 139

It's fun to break rules, but what about breaking rulers? Without the ruler, there is no judgement or comparison to the way it "should" be. Stop "shoulding" all over yourself, and don't let others "should" on you either! Pee-ew. Only you are in control of how your life is measured. Be confident in your skin, and allow others the same respect. By judging others, you only distract yourself long enough to avoid having to deal with an internal fear, like "shoulding" on yourself. Release all attachments to judgement and wipe your worries clean!

It is time for you to stop giving a fuck! You do not need validation or approval from anyone. Stop comparing yourself to other people. Breathe! Relax! Be the greatest version of yourself for YOU and nobody else. You are internally validated, gorgeous, and your self-esteem is impregnable. Never give a poo what anyone else thinks of you! You are the baddest MOFO in this wild universe. Your power is in how you choose to react.

Trudging through life as part of the negative goon squad will never reap a positive outcome. Any seed you plant will grow. If you plant negativity, you'll sprout negativity. If you plant positive vibes, you'll sprout positive vines. You know when you step in dogpoo without realizing it and then you smell it and immediately think it's some stinky bastard around you? Later, you get home, and realize it was you the whole time. It's easy to run around blaming the world for everything that stinks until you finally figure out it's just you. Instead of soiling your pants, confront your attitude and mindset. Plant a forest of positivity and build your dream house in it.

Life is a creative adventure to relentlessly improve your mind, body, and soul. It's supposed to be difficult and frustrating at times—that's the only way to learn and develop. If life wasn't difficult, you'd still be stinking up diapers and waiting for Grandma to come wipe your ass because it's easy. Take pride in hard times, and use the experiences to fuel your adventure.

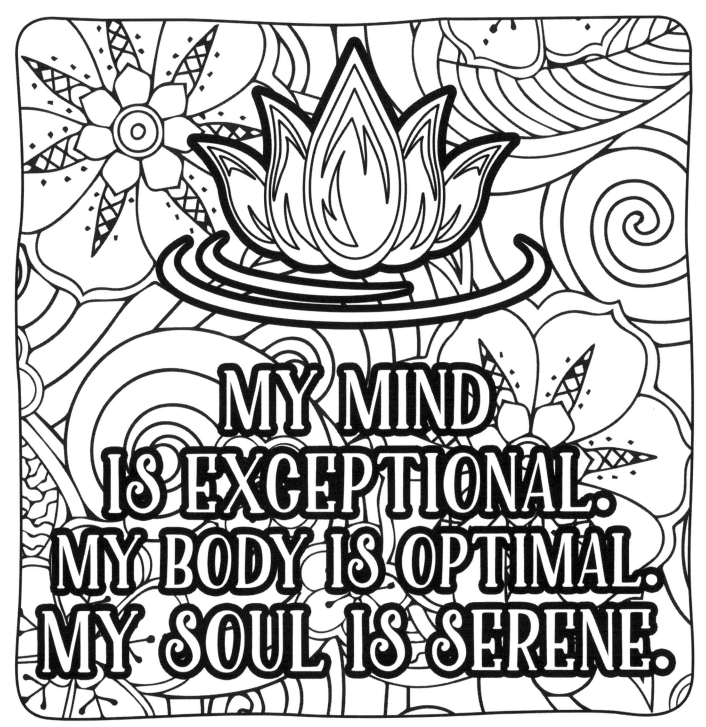

The American Dream

It's as depressing as a dimple on your butt.
If you behave you'll get a nickel you can spend
on some stuff.
And in time you'll get a dime if you impress your boss,
So you can buy some more junk just to numb
your thoughts.

Don't let this cycle consume your life as it does so many others. Chase your dreams and the money will follow. Chase money, and you may never catch your dreams. The purest measure of wealth is how much you are worth when you lose all your money. If you truly want to feel rich, count all the beauty in your life that money cannot buy. You may find the areas that matter the most are priceless!

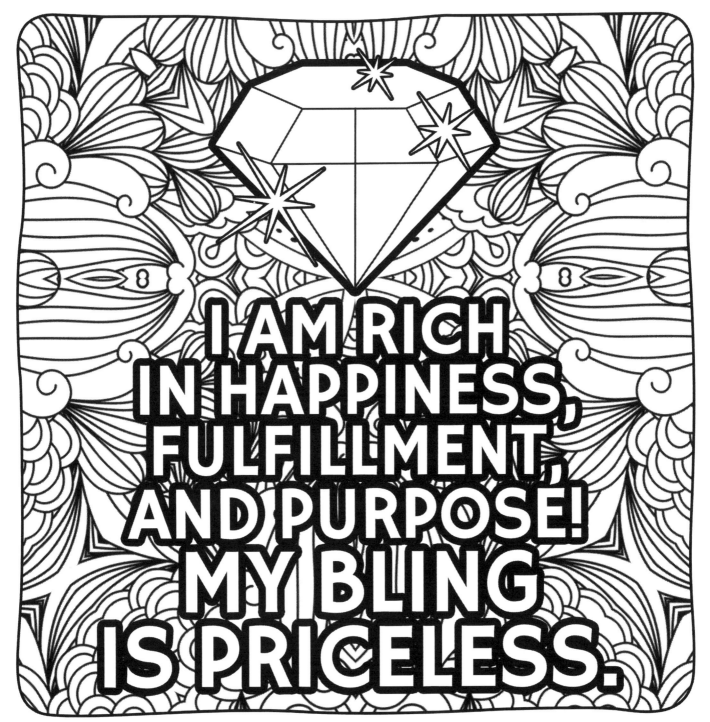

You are a brew of the gods, magic, and the impossible. You are a creation with as much wizardry as any in the universe.

You have the ability to move freely and explore. You have the gift of communication and choice. You were born equipped with a power that only gods have: the power to create.

It's the only power you need to manifest happiness and freedom forever!

Resistance gremlins sometimes surge in the form of insecurity. Unload your machine gun of confidence to defeat them!

When you believe in yourself, there is no need to convince others. Johnny might have bigger muscles and a sweet Fu Manchu, and Milly might have bathtubs full of Benjamins, but comparison is the thief of joy. Move forward with the confidence of a bare-ass toddler running around with his diaper on his head! When you love and accept your differences, the world will love and accept you.

You are alive. If that's not enough to make you raging ecstatic, then what is? You live in a world full of unlimited abundance and opportunity. You have magical senses to interact with your experience, and you DECIDE how you want to view it all. Wire your brain to focus on the positives, and you will only experience positives. Make sexy time with your optimistic side, and you will pop out optimistic babies to surround you the rest of your life.

You are an enchanting child of nature with extraordinary capabilities. You have a magical brain, heart and gut! You have 206 bones and 640 muscles in your body, along with other organs, ligaments, joints, arteries, tendons and tissues all working toward your function. Your senses allow you to experience the world. Be grateful for the small things in life, like the ability to wipe your ass and sleep through the night without pissing yourself.

Money is not the fountain of eternal happiness. Money only makes you more of who you are. If you are an asshole who loves to slay strip clubs, rail cocaine, and participate in a life of meaningless hoo-ha, money only allows you to do this on a larger scale. If you are a big-hearted philanthropist who loves to help the well-being of others, money allows you to help MORE people in BIGGER ways. You are not a slave to God Money. You are the God of Money. Use it to build your Kingdom of happiness and purpose, and your Kingdom shall be infinitely wealthy.

You aren't electronic.
You cannot plug into a wall and
re-energize. Your battery depends on the
great outdoors. Don't make the mistake
of letting technology rule your life.
Nature is your everlasting cure.

"Somewhere, some poor, phoneless fool is
probably sitting by a waterfall, completely
unaware of how pissed off he should be at
the world." -Duncan Trussell

Inside every one of us is a beauty and a beast. The beauty is a product of our joy, peace, love, humility, generosity, and compassion. The beast is a product of our jealousy, arrogance, ego, greed, regret, and sorrow.
Feed the beauty and not the beast.

When you get in line to have the fast food mascots serve shit to you on a tray, are you using your health and consciousness to their fullest capacities? To perform at your highest, you must feel your best inside and out. Treat your body with respect and optimal care, for it is the sanctuary that carries your sacred passenger.

Whatever it is that you want,
you must start giving it away.

If you want to learn something and change your life,
teach someone else a value that will change theirs.
If you want help to overcome an obstacle, start helping
others overcome theirs.
If you want to be loved, put on a Barry White album,
take some notes, and start loving others.
If you long for prosperity and abundance,
be grateful for your current fortune and share it with
one who has less.

The smallest gifts that you release will circle back
around with opportunity and abundance aimed
specifically for you.

The world influences our desires to crave higher quantities! More money. More sex. More friends. More followers. More cars. More undies! Sadly, higher quantities only create shallow satisfactions in the moment. To be truly happy, try befriending quality, not quantity. How can you take what is already part of your life to the next level? Instead of the job you hate that pays the most, how about one you love that pays enough? Instead of 20 Tinder dates a week with the world's best Photoshop con artists, how about 1 really strong transparent and beneficial relationship?

The anchors of your happiness are already part of your life. How can you crack open the magic within? It's time to put on the silk undies and ditch the rest!

Do you ever point the finger at all the madness around you and blame it for the shortcomings you experience?
What if you turned the finger towards yourself ? What would you find?
External madness can only affect you if you have internal voids that allow it in. When searching for faults, use a mirror and not a telescope. When you heal the shortcomings within, confrontation cannot enter.
When you block out unhappiness, all that's left is happiness.

You are a hunk of magical meat strapped to a skeleton made of stardust. You are raging through space on a giant rock at approximately 67,000 mph around a giant ball of fire in an infinite abyss. Be brave and bold in your quest, because you are a product of the impossible.

You are leveling up. You are gaining superpowers. You bust through brick walls and smash the skulls of fear gremlins around every corner. You fall off cliffs. You get attacked and eaten by monsters. But, you always show back up twice as strong, mentored by the wisdom of your wounds. Bust through the levels! Throw fireballs at all that resists, and blindside the boss who holds your passion hostage! Free the royalty within and conquer your creative empire. Be the last action hero.

You are living a movie. You are writing and producing the story. This world and everyone in it is your audience. Will people be excited to watch you gloriously slay the dragon at the summit of Mt. Fuckery, or will they be disappointed with a mundane and boring existence? Sitting on the couch with your hands down your pants while devouring a bucket of fried chicken DOES NOT change the world, and nobody wants to see that nastiness. Your life is an epic quest of awesome adventures and exploration. Strive to make it the most memorable movie possible.

By creating a vision, you set a focus for where you are heading in life. If you follow the direction of YOUR VISION, you will create the life of your dreams. If you fail to create your own vision, others will make it for you by placing ads, commercials, billboards, religions, politics, traditions, and spray tan machines around you. Do yourself a solid and define your future without outside influences! Believe, take relevant actions, and your vision will become your reality.

Ask the Universe for water and your
thirst will be quenched.
You are a magnet of your own blessings.
You know the essence of what you want
and you earn it. You are a fish in the water,
swimming in any direction you choose.
All visions that you support with your
highest intentions will come to pass.
Whatever you are reaching for, in return,
is reaching for you.
Be one with your calling.

Why, as humans, do we lock ourselves in cubicle cages and rage our energy on nonsense that in no way contributes to our happiness and freedom? No other species on earth is worried about a Facebook status, an urgent email from a boss, or that sleazy dress that Becky wore to the company dinner. Release your judgements, rediscover your relationship with momma earth, and run like a fucking antelope outta' control!

You are one energy with the world, and this experience of life is but a pulse in an infinite magical voyage. There is no difference of energy between your life, the life of a bee, the experience of an angel, or the workout moves of Richard Simmons. We are all the same, experiencing life through a perception, turned on for a period of time, and off for a period of time. A wave rises and breaks. A flower blooms and decays. All life is an energy rising together! Try not to trap your energy on desires of the self. Instead, use it for the highest good of all.

If you intend on creating the life you love, but you only focus your attention on muscle-beach speedo competitions or celebrity news feeds, your intention is powerless. If your attention is disciplined, but you have no intention for your vision, your mission is aimless. If you breed your attention with your intention, your visions will come to life. Pay attention to your intentions and the world shall be yours! Please don't use your new powers for manifesting speedo competitions.

Around 180 million semen warriors start the mighty race for reproduction when Cupid shoots his love arrow. They swarm through crowded villages, maze through tunnels, and battle through the great protectors in the Queen's ovary palace. For the few that make it through the marathon and past the guards, it usually takes teamwork to break down the fortress that protects the eggs of life. Once the fortress is cracked, only one victor can slip through and claim the prized egg! If you think you have no chance in bringing your dreams to life, remember that you are the result of Mother Nature's most impossible race. You are the genetic combination of the fiercest marathon warrior and the rarest prized egg of life. Victory is already yours.

When your weakness is exposed and you feel like a helpless donkey strapped to an operating table, remember that you aren't the first one to be diagnosed by the peanut gallery. In the sinking pits of despair, you must trek forward to the next great summit! Expose yourself and be transparent. Reflect the wisdom of your fall back into the world! The lowest points in life are preparing you for the next highest explorations! How high can you get? NEVER. STOP. PEAKING.

Sometimes when you fly, you get super high in the moment, and you're distracted by the sheer magnificence of the space that surrounds you. It's important to remember that you cannot tango with every passing asteroid if you wish to reach the stars. Always stay focused on what lights you up!
You were born to shine.

Easier said than done, right?
But, just like twerking, the more you do it, the easier it gets. You may even become addicted to the adrenaline of proving that nervous friend inside of your head wrong. That voice wants to protect you, but it also doesn't know how powerful you are.
All ships are safest at shore,
but that's not what ships are for!
Unfurl your sails and harness the wind!
An ocean of treasure awaits!

There is nothing more draining than allowing someone to offend you. If you let them under your skin, you are allowing them to suck out your beautiful energy and replace it with stress. If you ignore their ignorance, you can use the energy to distribute positivity throughout the rest of your day. The next time you are tempted to engage in offensive exchanges with someone who clearly has a stick up their booty, turn your cheek and flash a smile instead! Let the confrontations pass like gas! Your energy is for YOU, not them.

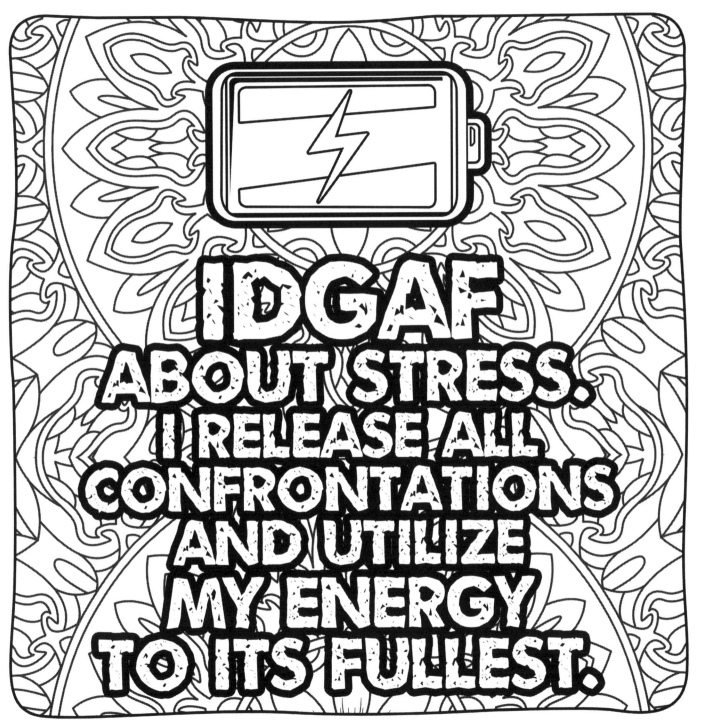

UNLEASHING
THE POWER OF CREATION

You are the blood of savages, warriors, knights, and raging maniacs that refused to quit. For millions of years your ancestors were hardcore fighters and survivors, and had ANY of them dropped dead before successfully reproducing, you wouldn't be here today. You are a golden goose with genes so powerful you can survive natural disasters, droughts, plagues, and wars. Armor up and swing your battle ax at any force that steps in the way of your creations.

Should you turn the alarm clock off and sleep instead of getting up early and working out? Should you give the checkout clerk a wedgie for putting cream in your coffee when you asked for black? Will you let the meltdown of your current situation paralyze you so you never create again? Hell nah! You are a conflict assassin, and you have the power to take it on the chest, deal with it like a boss, and accelerate your sweet ass life! You are in charge of all outcomes. Choose wisely!

Problems are our homies, our peeps, and our friends. There will always be problems, and this means there will always be new opportunities to creatively solve these problems! Opportunities open the door to unlimited possibility. Freedom is for those who solve the problems. Pacifiers are for those who don't.

File your fears into the fuck-it cabinet and show up to meet your muse. Opportunity is the direct result of creation. If you continue to create, you will continue to bring opportunity to life.
No matter how hard it feels, or how foggy your star quest looks, keep exploring the route! You may only be able to see what's directly in front of you, but you can still reach the stars that way.
A dance with the creative universe awaits!

You are a copy of a copy with magic on top. You are the product of a thousand generations, but unique in your angle. Don't be afraid to study and adopt the ideas, strategies, and creativity of others. All our creations are modifications of those before us with a slight burst of the magic within our personalities. Adding your unique twist to an existing idea is still a magical, pure form of creativity. Put on your disco pants and do a little dance with the shortcuts the world offers you! We'd all still be blobs of slime if we weren't supposed to learn, copy, and improve. What new angle can you add to the canvas of universal creativity?

Do you always finish what you are working toward? Do you launch your creations? It's easy to stop production when Mr. and Mrs. Comfort drop a treasure chest of attractive distractions in your lap. Sometimes resistance gremlins show up looking super sexy in an attempt to flatter your weakness! Deny those sneaky little gremlins, flip the rage create switch, and keep hustling! These comforts are a desperate surge from resistance in disguise! They are splits in the track to see if you can be derailed. Rage on! Overcome the weenies in disguise! Nobody ever won freedom by taking the bait.

The definition of success is "the accomplishment of an aim or purpose." Success is extremely subjective and never guaranteed! However, if you do not try, you have a 100% chance of failing. Nothing ventured, nothing gained! Alternately, if you never stop trying, you have a 100% chance of learning and experiencing something new. If you commit to learning and gaining new experience in the direction of your dreams, you'll fill your journey with success, happiness, freedom and purpose.

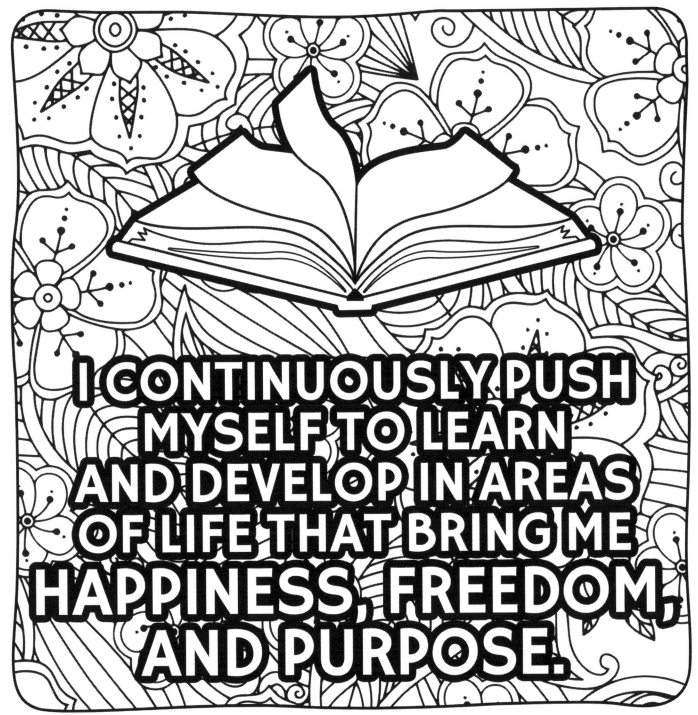

When you resist, you conform to the death of creation—the death of yourself.
When you create, you destroy resistance.
To manifest a life of pure happiness and freedom, you must create it.
Therefore, you must destroy resistance.
Those sneaky little resistance gremlin buffoons will never stop attacking,
but you can dismantle their army with continuous action.
Persistence is your sharpest weapon.
If you keep showing up, you will wear down your enemy.

Remove anything in your life that is not of absolute value. Clear the clutter in your home, your email inbox, and your social media accounts. The price of distraction is much greater than you think!

less distraction = more awareness = more focus on value = stronger relationships + higher levels of creativity = more opportunities = more success = happiness + freedom

Your distant ancestors didn't dick around worrying about how good they looked to the rest of the world. They were out hunting animals, battling enemies, and creating empires. They probably smelled like ass and were completely unaware that their descendants would gel their hair, shave their butts, and implant body parts to impress each other. Quit focusing on the surface and do what needs to be done in the core to survive and advance. The future depends on you.

Why settle for being a king when you can be a god? Why settle for watching someone else create their dreams when you can create your own? One day, you will physically expire, but this doesn't have to be the end of you. Everything you work on, create, and influence will continue to work, create, and influence after you jump ship. The world will absorb your flesh and become one with your sacred creations. What message do you want to leave?

You cannot become the person you dream of being by remaining who you are. Give your past a friendly slap on the ass and embrace the new direction of winds. With every choice that life presents, make the uncomfortable decision to explore the unknown. You are only free if nothing holds you back. You're a fucking superstar!

Everything that you do, do it so you FEEL it. Do it with pride and honor. If you sling hotdogs on the corner, sling the hell out of those weenies with extra kraut and mustard. If you clean out porta-potties at dingy music festivals, make those honey buckets shine like world class diamonds. The happiest of hippies awaits your masterpiece! Your work currently supports your life and helps put food in your stomach. Be thankful for the foundation you have as you work toward the next step in your freedom quest. You cannot launch a rocket without a launchpad.

Life isn't about waiting for handouts from everyone else. Life is about knowing what you want and going looney in your pursuit of it. People can be the most powerful asset in your arsenal, but if you aren't careful, they can also take control of your direction. If you start depending on others to let you suck the tit, it will only delay your ability to create independent growth. Create your own mission and objectives, and then surround yourself with a crew that will help your spaceship blast higher. Be thankful for the support, but always remember that you are in control of where your rocket is headed. You can choose any star you want.

The universe will always test your temper. It's the natural order of things. We've all had those days where a bird drops a fresh squeezer on our heads. For every positive, there is a negative. You can either allow these sour dips to cripple you, or you can laugh like a raging lunatic, take note of the lesson, and use the experience as motivation to dominate moving forward. Be patient. Be kind. Be that weird, freakishly happy maniac in the coffee shop. When life gives you lemons, paint those fuckers in gold, then feed them to the world.

When the thunder roars and you feel the chaos moving closer, proudly take guard and (wo)man the fucking storm! Bring on the lightning and the floods! Gear up in your finest shields and ships and parade to the center of the turmoil! Without the storms, your seeds cannot sprout! Without the storms, there cannot be growth! When life hits you in the face with a bag of shit, use it to fertilize the next generation of your creations. You can't calm the storm; you can only calm yourself. A settling of peace follows every black cloud. In this state of calmness, your finest creations will expand their roots and turn all the uproars into magical flowers.

It's easy to feel like happiness is elusive. You feel incredible and confident one day, and then unimportant, unattractive, and depressed the next. Before you know it, you end up slamming a bottle of wine and a tub of ice cream to help numb the gloom. But, just as people transition from unhealthy and overweight to healthy and fit, you can exercise your happiness muscle and build a life of smiles. With the tiniest practices of gratitude and mindfulness, and a focus on what truly lights you up, you can turn yourself into the Hulk Hogan of happiness. The army of sadness cannot break down your fortress if you are kicking their ass everyday.

There is only one bubble between you and your exciting, maniac visions. The size of the bubble depends on how much space you allow it to occupy. The more you let distraction, fear, and resistance gremlins bloat your bubble, the more distorted your view becomes. If you only knew the magic that awaits you on the other side, you would have popped that bubble a long time ago. The shortest distance between you and your vision is believing that you already have it and performing the part! When you play the role of your vision, there is no room for the space in between. Go HAM and pop it like it's hot!

You did not wake up to simply exist. This is your ONE LIFE, and it is the sum total of every moment you have ever experienced. Yesterday you may have been hit by a missile of fuckery so huge that your motivation was completely wiped from the universe. Yesterday is gone. Each second that you breathe is a bonus round to develop more excitement, adventure, and purpose in your life. Slow down and enjoy something beautiful. Not everyone has made it as far as you.

Do not make the mistake of simply existing as a hermit on the shore, sipping margaritas and never leaving the security of your shell. Kick it into beast mode and dive into the waters. You are the King of Tides. You are the Queen of Light. You are a maniac banshee doing backflips through the treetops of resistance. You are a battleship smashing through waves, exploring new lands, and digging up treasures buried deep beneath the comfort beaches. You have breakdowns. You have scars. But you also have wisdom of gold. You are truly alive and full of light.

So many people view life as an external lottery, hoping for the chance at a big payout that will solve all their problems. Meanwhile, they blow their earnings on junk and substances to numb how "unlucky" they are. The real lottery is 100% internal. If you consistently invest in yourself, and you take some risks out of your comfort zone, you WILL create your dream life. If you have a vision and you follow it, there is only one outcome. The persistent lion eats the lucky duck.

If you found out today that you had to live your EXACT same life all over again, how would you change it from this moment on? Sure, you may have experienced copious amounts of embarrassing fart moments, early-90's haircuts, and screwing things up in the past, but none of that matters because it cannot be changed. Move forward with an intent to experience the ultimate highs of life. Make decisions moving forward that you'd be ecstatic to revisit 10 times over! Live your life as if you had to live it all over again.

"When you follow your bliss, that thing that truly electrifies you, four things automatically happen: you put yourself in the path of good luck, you meet the people you want to know, doors open where there weren't doors before, and doors open for you that wouldn't open to anybody else." - Joseph Campbell

Electrify yourself. Follow those smiles!

How often do you take a break from the competitive sport of life and gaze into the sky? The gift of your life is a beautiful trophy and YOU get to cherish the treasure. During the day you are blessed with a giant ball of fire recharging your battery and lighting your way. Then you get to dance with dusk in her dark speckled dress under a million candles that guard you while you rest. Your next breath is much more valuable than your next paycheck. Don't get buzzed up in a lifelong competition to win the "Busiest Bee" trophy. The cost to play is awfully high, and you already have the ultimate prize!

Too many people leave guts on the floor as they crawl through the week like snails, wishing it was the weekend. How often do you think, "If only it was Friday..." and, "I can't wait for the weekend to get here!" When you wish away your week, you are wishing away your time. Wishing away your time is like inviting the Grim Reaper to your private dinner. Do you really want to wish away your family, your friends, and your ONE LIFE? Everything you take for granted is someone else's fairytale. Cherish each and every moment that you have before time makes you cherish what you had. Every day is a Saturday.

When you give something to another person, whether material or in service, a physiological response happens within you. A warm fuzzy feeling creeps in and helps you make sexy time with your happiness. Your brain releases pleasure endorphins, including oxytocin, which lowers stress. Oxytocin makes you feel more connected to others, which is why good deeds are often paid forward. The greatest gift to yourself is a gift to someone else. Pay it forward!

Up to this point, you may have aimlessly floated through life "searching" for happiness. You tried googling cat videos, binge drinking, occasional narcotics, strange sex, and even reality television. You tried to find the answers by asking your teachers, religious influences, co-workers, family and friends. DUDE! You have been searching for thrills and not happiness. Happiness is not something you can find—it's only something you can create. Close your eyes and visualize how your life looks when you are truly happy. What step can you take today to move toward your vision?

Today's world teaches us that if we prepare well enough, the future will satisfy our happiness. "Don't enjoy life now—save for retirement! Age 65 will be a perfect time to celebrate life!" WTF kind of goon squad advice is this? They're missing whole point! By constantly stressing about the future, your awareness is not fully there, or here. Eagerly preparing for your future comes with a price tag of anxiety, which destroys all advantages that foresight has to offer. Having a vision for personal development and who you wish to become is magical, but do not forget that development only happens in the moment. Develop within your experience!

You could have been an ant protecting your queen, or a leaf on a bush in the jungle. But you aren't. You are you. You are supposed to be you. You are superfly and sexy AF. Life is a discovery of yourself, and then a journey to help others discover their magic as well. What can you do today to get closer to the new you? How can this new you help those around you? Every day, ask yourself these questions:

How can I become 1% better?

How can I use my services to help another become 1% better?

We all face unexpected adversity in life. Loss of income. Illness in the family. Someone steals your Fruity Pebbles. These moments always sneak up when you least expect them, causing internal mayhem in the form of anxiety, depression, and even anger. Although Fruity Pebble theft should be punishable by lashings, what's done is done and cannot be changed. Accept your disposition and make the best of what comes next! For the rest of your life, your moments will ALWAYS turn out the best if you make the best of the way your moments turn out!

You are heating up. You are flaming hot. You are 360 slam-dunking on all resistance gremlins that stand in your way. Your focus is escalating. Your mind is a factory of awareness. Each night, you rest as a stronger, smarter, happier, and more meaningful person than you were at any other time in your life. May the best moments of your past be the worst of your future!

ACHIEVEMENT UNLOCKED: SHARE YOUR COLORED AFFIRMATIONS AND WIN!

Wohoo! Congratulations on coloring your way through the Sweet-Ass Affirmations coloring book.

You've just unlocked the opportunity to win some sweet-ass goodies!

How to Win

There are two ways to enter into our contests to win free affirmation decks and other Rage Create swag!

1. Take a creative picture or video of your favorite colored Affirmation page or card and **tag us on social media** @ragecreate on Instagram and Facebook or @Rage.Create on TikTok. You can also email your entry to hello@ragecreate.com.

2. **Leave us an honest review** about your experience with the Sweet-Ass Affirmations Coloring Book on Amazon (if you purchased it there) and send us a copy of the review to hello@ragecreate.com.

You'll get an extra entry everytime you share and/or leave a review.

If you purchased it on RageCreate.com, send your thoughts to us at hello@ragecreate.com.

You'll get an extra entry every time you share!

We also run occasional giveaways at RageCreate.com/Giveaway

Social Media Links

- Instagram: @ragecreate
- Facebook: @ragecreate
- TikTok: @Rage.Create

FREE BONUS PACK: SPECIAL OFFER FOR YOU

As a thanks for supporting this project, we've created a pack of free digital goodies for you, including:

- All 60 High-Resolution Affirmation Cards in Digital Format (front and back)
- Desktop and Mobile Wallpaper Backgrounds for Each Card!
- Print-at-home Affirmation Card Pack so you can make your own deck at home

DOWNLOAD YOUR FREE BONUS ITEMS HERE:
RAGECREATE.COM/COLORBONUS

OR SCAN THIS QR CODE:

20% off on your Sweet-Ass Affirmations Card Deck

We just can't help ourselves, so here are more treats! Here is a 20% off coupon to the *Sweet-Ass Affirmations: Motivation for Your Creative Maniac Mind* affirmation decks.

You can redeem at RageCreate.com:
Promo code:
COLORBONUS20

MORE MOTIVATION FOR YOUR CREATIVE MANIAC MIND

Available at RageCreate.com

Decks

Sweet-Ass Affirmations 1

60 Witty, Uncensored Affirmation Cards to Motivate Your Creative Maniac Mind

$22.00

Sweet-Ass Affirmations 2

The Sequel Deck that Raised $160k on Kickstarter - 60 More Cards to Help Unleash Your Creative Beast

$22.00

Mugs

Rebirth Mug

Forget the old you! Be reminded every morning of the absolute superstar you are becoming!

$19.99

Go the F*ck Outside Mug

Be reminded every morning to go out and soak up on Mother Nature's love!

$19.99

T Shirts

Rebirth (Light and Dark)

Reinvent yourself. And look absolutely cool in this shirt while you're at it!

$24.99

Go the F*ck Outside (Light and Dark)

Wear this epic shirt outdoors and spend quality time with Mother Nature!

$24.99

Check out all of our products at RageCreate.com

MEET THE RAGE CREATE TEAM

Heath

Co-founder and author
HeathArmstrong.com

Jason

Co-founder and design
JasonBerwick.com

Jo

Lead design

Lindsay

Support and management

Jan

Fulfilment and
e-commerce

Skid

Unisquid oracle

POWER AFFIRMATIONS FOR YOUR CREATIVE MANIAC MIND PODCAST

Do you love audio?

Check out the podcast for daily sweet-ass affirmations shared by our co-founder Heath with hype music and brief meditations.

RageCreate.com/podcast

Made in the USA
Columbia, SC
28 October 2022